So You Think You Know About Horses?

By the same author

Safety With Horses

Behind the Stable Door
Horse and Pony Care

The SR Direct Mail Book of Eventing
(with Alan Smith)

Twenty-Five Years in Show Jumping
(with David Broome)

Show Jumper

So You Think You Know About Horses?

Questions to test your knowledge

Brian Giles

Cartoons by Jake Tebbit

Stanley Paul
London Melbourne Sydney Auckland Johannesburg

Stanley Paul & Co. Ltd

An imprint of Century-Hutchinson Ltd

17–21 Conway Street, London W1P 6JD

Hutchinson Group (Australia) Pty.Ltd
16–22 Church Street, Hawthorn, Melbourne, Victoria 3122

Hutchinson Group (NZ) Ltd
32–34 View Road, PO Box 40-086, Glenfield, Auckland 10

Hutchinson Group (SA) Pty Ltd
PO Box 337, Bergvlei 2012, South Africa

First published 1985

© Brian Giles 1985

Illustrations © Jake Tebbit 1985

Set in Plantin by BookEns, Saffron Walden, Essex

Printed and bound in Great Britain by Anchor Brendon Ltd
Tiptree, Essex

British Library Cataloguing in Publication Data

Giles, Brian
So you think you know about horses?
1. Horses—Juvenile literature
I. Title
636.1'0076   SF302

ISBN 0 09 162331 6

Contents

Acknowledgements

My special thanks to Marion Paull who came up with the idea, to Judith Draper who read the manuscript and to Jake Tebbit whose marvellous cartoons grace many of the pages.

Foreword

by Lucinda Green

Brian Giles has been involved with horses for longer than I. His enthusiasm and interest have always been apparent and his desire to help out riders in difficulties is generally admired throughout the horse world.

His latest addition to the bookshelf provides a rare opportunity of learning through amusement and fun and the questions he poses will be enjoyed by anyone with an equine interest from the age of nine to ninety, be they onlookers or participants.

I can fully recommend this book as a means of acquiring knowledge without any of the discomfort normally associated with such a pursuit.

Introduction

One of the best ways to have fun and test your knowledge of horses is to try a quiz because it does test what you know to the full.

In this book I have covered a wide range of equestrian subjects, and even if you cannot answer all of the questions you will, I hope, find the exercise entertaining. One way to make it more fun is to see if you know more than your parents, brother or sister or friends. But winning is not really important, because the point of this book is for you not only to find out what you know but also to broaden your knowledge of equestrianism.

Some of the questions I have set are easy, some not so easy and some downright hard. But do not worry if you cannot answer a few of them because if you do not know, you can turn to the answers at the back of the book and find out for the future.

Instead of posing long questions, where possible I have deliberately kept them to one line so they are short and easily read and understood. In some cases the answers will just be a 'yes' or a 'no', giving you a chance to guess and find the correct solution. It heightens the fun.

Apart from questions on horse and pony management, there are also those on showjumping, eventing, dressage, racing, point-to-pointing, horses in history, polo, hunting and driving.

Learning is a vital part of life – it broadens your outlook and makes you more interesting as a person. I have always been a firm believer that education, in any sphere, must be made easier than it sometimes is and that, no matter what you are studying, it must also be fun. If it is, then the going gets that much easier.

That is why we have asked Jake Tebbit to draw some of his marvellous cartoons. I am sure you will enjoy them as much as I do. The quality of his work is extremely high, always hilarious and amply illustrates exactly what I mean when I say that it can be fun to learn.

The more you know about horses the better it is for them, too, because I am sure that much of what they suffer is due to ignorance on our part more than anything else. But many of you might not know about horses unless someone teaches you, so never be afraid to ask questions and read as much about the subject as you can. One of the joys of life is that you never stop learning, no matter how good you are or how much you know.

I hope, in some small way, this book will help further your knowledge and understanding of horses and those who ride them. It would give me a great deal of pleasure if you enjoy this book as much as I did putting it together.

Practical Questions

Stable management 1

1 What does a horse feed from in his stable?
2 What does he sleep on?
3 Should the floor of the stable be level or have a slight slope?
4 What do you call removing soiled straw from the stable?
5 What is the term for cleaning a horse?
6 What is the name of the brush used for taking off dried mud?
7 Should you use it on your horse's face?
8 With what do you remove stones from the shoes?
9 What does a stabled horse usually wear in winter?
10 When you take a horse's temperature, where do you put the thermometer?

Stable management 2

1 What is the term for filing a horse's teeth?
2 Who puts the animal's shoes on?
3 Which is the odd one out – dandy brush, body brush, hoof pick?
4 On what part of the pony would you find a frog?
5 How many inches in a hand?
6 What is it called when your horse moves its head from side to side over the stable door?
7 What is the equestrian term for a horse's left leg?
8 What is thrush?
9 A wisp is used for what?
10 What is between the fetlock and the coronet?

Stable management 3

1 What are molars?
2 What do you call a colt or filly who is 12 months old?
3 A full horse is called what?
4 What is the hair called that hangs from the horse's neck?
5 When you measure a horse or pony what unit of measurement do you use?
6 Has a body brush soft or hard bristles?
7 How do you tell the age of a horse?
8 Complete this saying 'No foot _____ _____'?
9 What is used to freeze-brand a horse?
10 What is a male horse called from six months to the age of three?

Stable management 4

1 Is it wrong to tie a horse up by his bridle?
2 Where would you find a horse's feathers?
3 What is the term for a castrated horse?
4 What is the maximum height for a pony?
5 What is the equestrian term for a horse or pony who eats everything that is put in front of him?
6 What are the two main types of shoeing?
7 Who uses a drawing knife?
8 Should you tie the rope from a horse's or pony's headcollar straight on to the stable ring?
9 Complete this phrase: salt-l_____.
10 What is a horse's normal temperature?

Stable management 5

1　Should electric light switches be inside or outside the stable?
2　Should a haynet be placed above the horse's head?
3　Why should stable floors slope slightly?
4　With what knot do you tie a horse's headcollar rope?
5　Why is hoof oil put on horses' feet?
6　Name the three types of straw sometimes used for horses' bedding.
7　Which is considered the best of the three to use?
8　What do you call the container for removing droppings?
9　Where do you put stable waste?
10　With what do you keep a horse's stable rug in place?

Stable management 6

1　Should you leave a tail bandage on for more than a few hours?
2　Why are tail bandages used?
3　What should you do with the horse's winter clothing in the summer?
4　Complete this item of grooming kit: curry _____.
5　What is a stable rubber used for?
6　When you return from a ride what is one of the first things you should do?
7　With what do you make a wisp?
8　Should you use a dandy brush on a horse's tail?
9　Where do you stand when washing the animal's tail?
10　When you are grooming what do you do with the eyes, nostrils and dock?

Stable management 7

1 How wide should the door of a pony's loosebox ideally be?
2 Why is the stable door in two halves?
3 Should the stable drain ideally be inside or outside the box?
4 In the evenings, when you tidy up the horse's bed and remove the droppings, you call it what?
5 When a horse has a haircut what is it called?
6 What is it called when you thin out a horse's mane?
7 When the mane is clipped off completely what is that called?
8 Complete this phrase: bran m _____.
9 When feeding carrots to a horse or pony how should they be cut?
10 Why?

Stable management 8

1 Should you keep a horse's food in tin or sack containers?
2 Who uses a buffer?
3 When a horse lies down in its box and cannot get up what is it called?
4 To prevent a horse slipping what are sometimes fitted to the underside of the shoes?
5 What keeps the horse's shoes in place?
6 What is the term for making a shoe?
7 Can tight shoes cause corns in a horse?
8 When you are mucking out what are the three items you must have?
9 Why is the stable floor left bare for a short while after mucking out?
10 How often should you muck out?

Stable management 9

1 A horse is measured from ground level to where?
2 When a horse has its hair cut off all over what is it called?
3 How often should a horse be shod?
4 Why should the doors of the stable open outwards?
5 What else can a horse live in, besides a stable?
6 Should the light bulbs in a stable be covered?
7 What is an entire?
8 What is chaff?
9 Is salt an essential part of a horse's diet?
10 Do some horses sleep on newspaper?

Stable management 10

1 Why should humans talk to horses?
2 What is deep litter?
3 When feeding a horse a titbit how should you do it?
4 What does conformation mean?
5 In equestrian terms what is the offside?
6 What are tushes?
7 When a horse bites his manger and sucks in air what is he called?
8 Ideally which direction should a stable face?
9 How many teeth should an adult horse have?
10 What is another word for strenuous grooming?

Grass-kept horses and ponies 1

1 Which plant is more dangerous to horses dead than alive?
2 If there were four horses in a field, how many feed bins should there be in that field?
3 When you have been working a horse which lives out what must you do before turning him out to graze?
4 What sort of rug does a horse wear when he is turned out in winter?
5 When you ride a pony who lives out should you give him a thorough grooming, or just remove the worst of the mud from his coat?
6 Why?
7 What should you take with you when going to catch your pony in his field?
8 What else is it best to take?
9 Apart from food and water, what else will your pony need in his field?
10 What must you do when you have led your horse or pony into the field?

Grass-kept horses and ponies 2

1 If a horse is living out and not being ridden, should you still have his feet trimmed?
2 In winter what should you do with the water bucket in the field?
3 Who needs more food, a horse who lives out or one who lives in?
4 What can a pony develop if he eats too much lush grass in the spring?
5 How can you arrange your grazing so that the horse doesn't graze the entire field?

6 What is one way of preventing worm re-infestation of the grass-kept pony?
7 Should you pick out a horse's or pony's feet daily if he is living out?
8 Why should you go and catch your pony daily?
9 Should you clip a pony who lives out in winter?
10 If a pony is not being ridden daily and lives out what should you check his coat for regularly?

Grass-kept horses and ponies 3

1 Which of these three should you not build paddock fences with: wood, plastic railing, barbed wire?
2 Is it wise to put cattle in with horses?
3 Why?
4 Why should you check your horse in the field before leaving for home?
5 What should you do before winter with a New Zealand rug, apart from checking that it does not have any holes in it?
6 Is it wise to turn your horse or pony out wearing a headcollar?
7 What is the name sometimes given to horse thieves?
8 What is the accepted amount of land one horse needs to graze upon, if the grass is plentiful?
9 When feeding hay to several horses in a field, what should you do with it?
10 Why?

Grass-kept horses and ponies 4

1 Is yew poisonous to horses?
2 What should you do with ragwort?
3 When you have been riding a grass-kept pony and he returns home warm, with sweat patches, which part of him should you dry first?

4   What are two of the most important facts you must remember when putting up or using a shelter for a horse, apart from its being constructed safely?

5   How do you encourage a horse or pony to use a shelter in wet or snowy weather?

6   If you found acorns in your horse's field what should you do with them?

7   Apart from keeping each other company, what else do horses do for each other which is very important?

8   When sectioning off an area of field, what is one of the easiest and most effective types of fencing to use?

9   What are the leg straps on a New Zealand rug designed to prevent?

10 The straps are made of leather. What is the New Zealand rug itself made of on the outside?

Grass-kept horses and ponies 5

1   Why should you always make a point of walking around a field where your horse is being kept?

2   If there was a stream with water running through the field would you allow your horse to drink from it?

3   When turning your horse out would you walk slowly into the field and gently slip off the headcollar, or turn him to face you, make a big fuss about it and encourage him to gallop off?

4   If you have just bought a horse or pony and you take him away and turn him out into your field why, for the first few weeks, must you take particular care and make sure you check on him several times a day?

5   Why do you have to make regular checks on him anyway, even when he has got used to his new home?

6   If your horse is constantly bullied by another in the field, what should you do?

7 Why should you give your horse a thorough examination daily?

8 In the winter, when there is very little goodness in the grass, with what should you supplement his diet?

9 After you have ridden your grass-kept pony should you turn him out straightaway if he is hot and sweaty?

10 Why should you always carry the number of your local vet?

Saddlery 1

1　What is another name for saddles and bridles?
2　What do you use to keep the bridle and saddle supple?
3　How many rings has an Irish martingale?
4　Complete the name of this famous make of saddle: S_____.
5　A whip is often described as a _____?
6　What is the name of the aid you hold in your hand?
7　How would you describe the top of the saddle at the front?
8　To what are the stirrup irons attached?
9　What is the back of the saddle called?
10　In what do you put the stirrup leathers to keep them in place?

Saddlery 2

1　In what do you put your feet when sitting in the saddle?
2　What has a child's safety stirrup fixed to it on either side?
3　When the saddle padding loses its filling what do you have to do with it?
4　What is the channel called which runs underneath the saddle from the front to the back?
5　If the saddle creaks and bends easily what might it have wrong with it?
6　If a saddle can be bent slightly and does not make a noise, what is the saddle likely to be called?
7　What are the hinged metal pieces attached to the stirrup bars called?
8　Name the pad which you put under the saddle.
9　What keeps the saddle in place?
10　When placed on the horse's back your saddle should be what?

Saddlery 3

1 When cleaning your tack should you use hot water or tepid water to wash off the mud?
2 When drying tack is it wise to put it on a radiator?
3 Why should you check your saddle and bridle daily?
4 What is the place called where you leave your saddle and bridle?
5 You might rest your saddle on a rack or a what?
6 What are the three main types of bit?
7 What is the piece of tack which fits behind the ears and over the poll?
8 What is a Kimblewick?
9 What is an Irish martingale?
10 What prevents the bridle slipping forward over the horse's ears?

Saddlery 4

1 What are the three types of martingale?
2 What is a Balding?
3 Do you know what a bridoon is?
4 What is a hackamore?
5 What is the function of a 'drop' noseband?
6 The running martingale is attached by rings to the bridle when fitted. It is also fixed to what?
7 What is the principal function of the breastplate?
8 Do you know what a crupper is used for?
9 A Kineton is a what?
10 What is a Grakle?

Riding technique 1

1 How many beats are there to the canter?
2 When you are cantering on a circle to the left, which leg should your horse be leading with?
3 What is the term for a very long-striding trot?
4 How many beats are there to the walk?
5 What does lateral mean?
6 When riding, your hands and legs can be described as?
7 When your horse is well on the bridle and up to its bit at a walk, what is it called?
8 Name the four kinds of canter.
9 How many beats are there to the trot?
10 What is it called when a horse or pony at canter switches from leading with his near-fore to his off-fore?

Riding technique 2

1 What is the purpose of riding a figure-of-eight?
2 What is the term used for asking a horse to move backwards?
3 When a horse stops at a jump what is it known as?
4 What is the name given to training fences which rest on a cross-section at each end of a pole?
5 What is it called when the print of a horse's hind foot falls exactly into the print of the forefoot?
6 When you are going over a jump and one arm is thrown in the air, what is it called?
7 When approaching a jump a horse must be?
8 When a horse changes from one pace to another, what is it called?
9 If a horse does not obey your commands what is it known as?
10 When first teaching a horse to jump should you gallop, walk or trot over the pole on the ground?

Riding technique 3

1 Should your elbows be in or out when riding?
2 When a horse makes a slight mistake on landing over a jump and his head nods, what is it called?
3 If a horse hesitates at a jump and springs from the ground with all four feet at once, what is it called?
4 When a horse runs alongside a fence and around it, what is it called?
5 Should a horse's back be flat when he jumps?
6 What is it called when a horse puts in a much bigger leap than is needed to clear an obstacle?
7 What does it mean when a horse 'puts in a short one'?
8 Should your heels be up or down when riding?
9 Should a rider hold on to his horse's mane when jumping to balance himself?
10 What can a novice rider put his fingers around to steady himself?

Before and after a ride 1

1 Should you groom your horse before tacking up for a ride?
2 What else should you remember to check?
3 What should you do with the stirrup leathers before walking your mount out through the stable door?
4 When you have mounted, what should you check before moving off?
5 What is the most important item you should wear when you ride?
6 What should that vital item also have attached to it?
7 What do these items do for you?
8 Should you ever mount a horse without them?
9 Why should you make sure that when you mount your horse is standing on a level surface?
10 Is it a good idea to vault into the saddle?

Before and after a ride 2

1 How do you measure the length of your stirrup leathers before mounting?
2 When mounted what should your stirrup leathers be?
3 From which side of the horse should you mount?
4 What is it called when somebody helps you into the saddle?
5 Before mounting you should check that your girths are not what?
6 Apart from climbing into the saddle yourself without aid, what else can you use to make it easier?
7 When you have put the bridle on your horse you should make sure that the bit is what?
8 You should also check that the throatlash and noseband are not too what?
9 Which way should you be facing when you begin to mount?
10 How many movements would you say there are when mounting?

Before and after a ride 3

1   If your horse returns to the stable hot and sweaty after his exercise, what should you do?
2   If he does return in a hot condition, should you allow him to drink cold water?
3   Is it necessary to pick out his feet when returning from a ride?
4   What do you call it when you put straw under the rug to help dry your horse off?
5   What part of the bridle should you always clean after use?
6   Why should you check your pony over when returning from a ride?
7   When you have dried your horse or pony, and he has settled down, what must you make sure that he has in his box?
8   If your horse returns from his ride hot and lives in a field, do you turn him out at once?
9   When you turn him out with what do you lead him?
10 If you turn him out in winter what should he be wearing?

Safety 1

1 In England, on which side of the road should you ride?
2 If a young novice horse and an older more experienced one are being ridden on the roads together, which one should be on the inside?
3 If riding at night or when the light is failing, what should you be wearing on your front and back?
4 What should you have on your stirrup irons?
5 When turning right, you look behind and put your right arm out at what height?
6 If you want a motorist to stop in front of you, how do you signal him to do so?
7 When walking in indian file along the road what distance should you keep from the horse in front?
8 When leading a horse on the road what should he be wearing?
9 If the road you are riding on is slippery, what should you do?
10 On narrow roads how should several riders ride?

Safety 2

1 When riding on roads should you hold a conversation with the person next to you?
2 How do you ask traffic to slow down?
3 What should you do when reaching a cross-roads?
4 On roads should you allow your horse to amble along on a loose rein?
5 If you want to turn left, what do you do?
6 When drivers slow down to pass you what should you do?
7 Should you trot downhill?
8 If riding up a very steep hill, what should you do?
9 If riding down a very steep hill what should you do?
10 Why should you not gallop on grass verges alongside roads?

Safety 3

1 Before riding on roads what should you first learn?
2 Should you give way to pedestrians at zebra crossings?
3 When you open a gate while out riding, what should you do afterwards?
4 When a horse is frightened of something what is it likely to do?
5 Should you ride across a field where crops are growing, or keep to the edges?
6 Should you keep to bridlepaths or ride anywhere you like?
7 When cantering along a designated riding area what should you always watch out for?
8 Why should you leave a gap between yourself and the horse in front?
9 How should you behave to drivers at all times?
10 What should you give drivers and other road users at all times?

Safety 4

1 On which side of the road should you lead a horse?
2 When you are leading a horse along the road should he be wearing a headcollar or a bridle?
3 When you are leading a horse in a bridle what must you not do with the reins?
4 If you have a horse who does not like traffic, should you ride him on a major highway?
5 If you were riding along the road and somebody wanted you to stop so that they could hold a conversation with you, would you stop or would you carry on?
6 Should you ride on the pavement?

7   If a motorist is going along the road and wants to turn right he signals, pulls out to the centre of the road and makes the turn when it is all clear. Does a rider do the same?

8   When riding around a roundabout which route should you take?

9   If you are passing another rider on a bridleway should you walk, trot or canter past?

10 Should you ride horses anywhere while wearing headphones and listening to pop music or anything else?

Ailments 1

1 If the frog smells badly what could the horse be suffering from?
2 What causes it?
3 If your mount's shoes do not fit correctly and pinch, what could it cause?
4 When a horse has stomach ache, what is it likely to be?
5 What is poll evil?
6 What is the name of the condition which can be caused by a horse being continually exposed to wet, muddy conditions?
7 If you allow your horse to stuff himself with rich spring grass, it could lead to his suffering from what?
8 Where does he get it?
9 What does sand crack affect?
10 What do all horses suffer from beginning with w?

Ailments 2

1 Which is the worst type of worm which attacks horses?
2 What is the first thing you should do when you discover that your horse has a contagious complaint?
3 When thinking about medication for horses, what should you always have at the stables?
4 What is sweet itch?
5 What is a bog spavin?
6 When a hind foot strikes a foreleg what is it called?
7 When one or both hind legs suddenly are snatched up very high when the horse moves, what is it called?
8 When a horse with a breathing problem has something inserted in his neck i.e. is given a tracheotomy, what else can it be called?
9 If a horse makes a noise when breathing heavily after working, what might he be?
10 If a horse has his testicles removed what is he known as?

Ailments 3

1 If your horse bruised his pedal bone from what might he suffer?
2 What causes a horse to suffer from sore shins?
3 What are windgalls?
4 Your horse should have a regular _____ injection?
5 Can horses catch flu?
6 If your horse has raised circular patches of hair on his neck and shoulders, what might he be suffering from?
7 Lampas is a condition found where?
8 What is a warble?
9 What part of the horse's body is affected by strangles?
10 What are bots?

Ailments 4

1 What is a splint and where would you find it?
2 In what part of the horse would you find canker?
3 Why must a horse or pony have its shoes replaced at intervals of between four and six weeks?
4 Where would you find a pedal bone?
5 What is the best treatment for sprains?
6 When a pony has laminitis how does the hoof differ in appearance from a healthy hoof?
7 When a pony has laminitis does he normally have heat in the front part of the feet?
8 If a horse has flu what must you do so that other horses will not become infected?
9 What parts of the horse does azoturia, also known as Monday-morning disease, affect?
10 What can you use as a poultice if you do not have a manufactured one at hand?

Travelling 1

1 If your horse was going on a journey in a vehicle, what might you put on his legs to protect them?
2 What might you put on his head in the horsebox if he is nervous or head shy?
3 What must you make sure you do along the way when taking your horse on a long journey?
4 Should you carry a water container with you even though you are only going on a short journey to a show?
5 Unless a horse hates flying, why is it better to send him by air than by road or sea?
6 If a horse becomes upset on a plane journey what might the vet give him to calm him down?
7 When travelling a horse by road the inside of the horsebox must have what?
8 What might you put on your horse's tail when travelling to prevent him rubbing it?
9 What must you not do with a tail bandage?
10 Should you load a sweaty horse into its box and then travel it?

Travelling 2

1 What do you pull down from your trailer to allow your horse entry?
2 What is it important to do when you have pulled down the answer to question 1?
3 Which way should a horse be facing in the trailer when it is travelling?
4 If a horse refuses to enter the horsebox or trailer what can you do to encourage him to enter?
5 If he still refuses to go in what might you ask your helpers to put around his quarters, well above the hocks?

6 What is the best solution for a horse who jumps off the side of the ramp as you try to load him?
7 How should your trailer be driven, particularly when your horse is inside?
8 Should you personally travel in the trailer with your horse?
9 Name the rug which horses sometimes travel in which deliberately has holes in it?
10 What will help to keep your horse contented while travelling?

Vices 1

1 If your horse gallops off with you, out of control, what do you say he is doing?

2 What do you call it when your mount stands up on his hind legs?

3 If your horse continually chews his headcollar rope and undoes the knot, what can you use instead to tie him up with?

4 If your horse has a habit of eating any type of bedding you put down for him, what is one way of preventing him from doing it?

5 If your horse keeps nipping at you, what should you do to try and stop him?

6 What is the most common reason for horses developing 'vices'?

7 Why do most horses hate being on their own and get up to mischief when they are left for long periods in a field without company?

8 When a horse or pony tries to get down when you are on his back what is he likely to be trying to do?

9 If your horse or pony is being naughty when you are riding him what must you never lose?

10 If your horse continually bites the horse next door what might he have to wear for a short period?

Food 1

1 Before feeding linseed what must you do with it?
2 Complete this saying: 'Feed little and _____.'
3 Why are horses fed chaff?
4 When would you feed your horse or pony a bran mash?
5 Why is it not a good idea to feed ponies a lot of oats?
6 When your horse has had plenty of time to eat his feed, what should you do if he leaves some in the manger?
7 What may cubes be substituted for?
8 With what would you associate sanfoin?
9 Hay which you feed to horses should smell s_____?
10 Has a horse a large stomach or a small one?

Food 2

1 What should you always do with dried sugar-beet pulp before feeding it to your horse?
2 Are peas and beans fattening to horses?
3 What should you do with peas and beans before feeding them to your horse?
4 What are rye and foxtail?
5 From what do you make hay?
6 When talking about horse food, with what would you associate the words seed and meadow?
7 If you wanted to change your horse's diet would you do it quickly or gradually?
8 What should you do with a horse's manger every day after he has eaten?
9 What does a horse need to maintain growth of his tissue and to keep him healthy?
10 Should you work a horse who has just eaten a big feed?

Competition Questions

Showjumping 1

1 When did David Broome win a World Championship?
2 Has Harvey Smith ever won a world title?
3 Name Harvey Smith's two sons.
4 Which one of them rode in the Los Angeles Olympics?
5 What medal did he win?
6 Name the non-riding British showjumping team captain for Los Angeles.
7 Who was the British showjumping team trainer in Los Angeles?
8 Name the horse John Whitaker rode in the Los Angeles Olympics.
9 Who won the Hickstead Jumping Derby in 1984?
10 On what horse did Eddie Macken win four Hickstead Derbies? (He has the same name as something aborigines throw which returns to them.)

Showjumping 2

1 In what year did the Royal International Horse Show move to the National Exhibition Centre in Birmingham?
2 Complete this man's name, Raymond Brooks-
3 Is the World Cup final an indoor competition or an outdoor one?
4 Who is known as the Master of Hickstead?
5 How many faults are given for one refusal?
6 What is the famous grassy mound called at Hickstead?
7 Complete this famous showjumping trainer's name, Ted E_____.
8 Who started riding Apollo after Geoff Glazzard?
9 Who used to ride Stroller?
10 Where is the Horse of the Year Show held?

Showjumping 3

1 Who rides Towerlands Anglezarke?
2 Has Captain Mark Phillips ever ridden showjumping?
3 What is the name of Captain Phillips's home?
4 What nationality is Paul Darragh?
5 Who rides Forever?
6 To whom is she married?
7 Where are the Pre-Wembley Everest Showjumping Championships held?
8 When a rider knocks a single pole down in showjumping how many faults does he incur?
9 Where is the Devil's Dyke jump?
10 Complete this lady's name: Pat Koechlin-S_____.

Showjumping 4

1 What nationality is Gerd Wiltfang?
2 On what horse did he win the World Championship in 1978?
3 Where did the World Championships that year take place?
4 Name the lady who used to ride Psalm.
5 Where were the 1972 Olympics held?
6 Who used to ride Mattie Brown?
7 What county does that rider come from?
8 In 1978 a horse called Claret won the King George V Gold Cup. Was the rider German, English or Australian?
9 Who used to ride Sportsman?
10 Name Harvey Smith's sponsors.

Showjumping 5

1 Name the horse on whom the late Caroline Bradley won the Queen Elizabeth Cup in 1978.
2 Who set the British high-jump record at Olympia in the same year?
3 How high did he jump?
4 What horse did he ride?
5 Complete this famous equestrian commentator's name: Dorian _____.
6 In what country is Calgary?
7 Who won the Olympic team showjumping in Los Angeles in 1984?
8 What famous showjumper from Germany has the initials H.W.?
9 In what county does Graham Fletcher live?
10 What is an oxer?

Showjumping 6

1 How many faults for a fall of horse or rider?
2 In which country does Gary Gillespie live?
3 What does FEI stand for?
4 At which show is the Queen Elizabeth Cup competition held?
5 Complete this rider's name: Michael M _____.
6 Name the two showjumping sisters whose family live in Essex and whose surname begins with B.
7 Who is the showjumping rider who regularly commentates on the sport for television?
8 What do you call the area where the horse waits before competing?
9 Who is the showjumping correspondent of the *Daily Express*?
10 Complete the name of this show: Bath _____?

Showjumping 7

1 What showjumping horse carries the name of a famous opera star?
2 For what famous stable did Lesley McNaught ride?
3 What nationality is Thomas Frühmann?
4 Where does Kevin Bacon come from?
5 Who is Secretary General of the British Show Jumping Association?
6 Who rides Mister Vee?
7 Where will the 1988 Olympic equestrian events be held?
8 If a showjumping rider finishes third in the individual Olympic showjumping what kind of medal does he/she win?
9 Name the horse Conrad Homfeld rode in the Los Angeles Olympic Games.
10 Who is the German rider who partners Palma Nova?

Showjumping 8

1 What team won the Aga Khan Nations Cup in Dublin in 1984?
2 Complete the name of this show in Germany: Donau_____.
3 Where does the Kent County Show take place?
4 Who retired as President of the British Horse Society in 1984?
5 When was showjumping first staged in the Olympic Games?
6 Complete this rider's name: Jean G_____.
7 What was the name of the famous grey horse David Broome retired at Olympia in 1983?
8 Name the two horses David Bowen took to the Los Angeles Games, but did not ride there.
9 In what county does David Bowen live?
10 Where is the Royal Show held?

Showjumping 9

1 There is a top-class lady showjumper from Switzerland with the initials H.R. What is her name?
2 What nationality is Rodney Jenkins?
3 How many Olympic gold medals has Hans Winkler won?
4 Where does he come from?
5 There are two famous brothers connected with showjumping who live in the answer to question 4 – who are they?
6 What chain of fashion stores sponsors John and Michael Whitaker and one of those well-known brothers?
7 What nationality is Ferdi Tyteca?
8 Who was the horse with a composer's name who helped David Broome win a World Championship?
9 How many children has David Broome?
10 Broome's sister is Liz who?

Showjumping 10

1 What is the main difference between the Hickstead shows and those held at Wembley?
2 Who is the Austrian rider who competes on Gladstone?
3 For what country does the great Deister compete?
4 Graziano Mancinelli won the individual gold medal in the 1972 Munich Olympics – where does he come from?
5 Complete the name of this competition – Nations C_____.
6 The best three scores for each team in each round count in the answer to question 5, but how many riders from one nation can actually take part in the competition?
7 Each team is allotted a certain number of points each season depending on their individual team results. What does the team who has the most points actually win at the end of the year?
8 Complete this horse's name: The Mav_____.
9 He was ridden by Alison D_____?
10 Complete the name of this competition: Take Your _____.

Showjumping 11

1   Who is the blind man who did so much for the sport of showjumping?
2   Does time count in showjumping competitions?
3   From what country do Raimondo and Piero D'Inzeo come?
4   Complete this man's name: Ted W_____.
5   For what country did Bill Steinkraus ride?
6   What is the name given to the class in which horses jump a very high wall?
7   Do ladies and men have separate World Showjumping Championships?
8   These two young men are showjumping brothers who live in Essex. Their first names are Mark and Phillip. Who are they?
9   If you got too near this German showjumping horse, maybe you would get burnt. He won a World title. What is his name?
10 Name the famous insurance company which is involved with showjumping's high-jump competitions and whose initials are N.U.

Showjumping 12

1   Where were the 1985 European Showjumping Championships held?
2   What was the famous horse Colonel Sir Harry Llewellyn used to ride?
3   Who won ten events at Wembley's Horse of the Year Show in 1984?
4   Did that rider win the Grand Prix Championship on the final day?
5   Where is the major pre-Christmas show in London held?

6 For which famous wine company does Essex rider Zoë Bates ride?

7 Name the double-glazing company which has done so much for showjumping in this country.

8 Who won the showjumping individual silver medal at the 1972 Munich Olympics, riding Psalm?

9 How many European Showjumping Championships has David Broome won?

10 Where was the 1985 Volvo World Cup Final held?

Showjumping 13

1 Name the showjumping correspondent of the *Daily Telegraph*.

2 David Vine is a famous sports personality for which TV station?

3 Complete this show's name: Three C_____.

4 In what county is the Towerlands Equestrian Centre?

5 Complete this rider's name: Michael W_____.

6 Has Emma Jane Brown ever won the Ladies' National Show-jumping Championship at Windsor?

7 Is the South of England Show at Ardingly an agricultural show?

8 Complete this man's name: General Sir Cecil B_____.

9 Complete this German rider's name: Peter L_____.

10 What nationality is Philippe Rozier?

Eventing 1

1   When a horse makes a mistake and either falls or refuses at an event what is he given?
2   What is the first phase of a three-day event called?
3   What is the final phase called?
4   Before any horse can take part in a three-day event, what does it have to pass?
5   If it fails the answer to question 4, it is what?
6   How many penalties are awarded for a first refusal across country?
7   How many refusals can a horse have at one fence across country before being eliminated?
8   How many time penalties are given for each second over the time allowed in the showjumping phase of a three-day event?
9   In which order do riders go in the showjumping phase?
10 Where are the Badminton Horse Trials staged?

Eventing 2

1   Badminton is a world famous venue for horse trials. Do you know when the first event actually took place there?
2   The man who runs Badminton used to be a well-known rider. What is his name?
3   Name the rider who has won Badminton more times than any other competitor.
4   How many times?
5   What was her maiden name?
6   She first shot to fame on a horse called what?
7   The lady married an Australian rider. What is his name?

8 When she won the World Championship in Luhmühlen in 1982 which horse did she ride?
9 After she won the World title a company based in London sponsored her. Name that company.
10 Who usually presents the Whitbread Trophy to the winner of Badminton?

Eventing 3

1 Miss Sheila Willcox won Badminton three times in the fifties, twice as Miss Willcox and once as Mrs _____?
2 In 1974 Captain Mark Phillips won Badminton on a horse owned by the Queen. What was it called?
3 How many times has Captain Phillips won Badminton?
4 Richard Meade first won Badminton on The Poacher in 1970. In 1982 he won the event again – on which horse?
5 In 1969 Pasha won Badminton and the rider created history by being the youngest competitor to win the event. What is his name?
6 What is the name of the family associated with Badminton?
7 Who are the main sponsors of the Badminton Horse Trials?
8 Name the New Zealand rider who won Badminton on Southern Comfort in 1980.
9 Jane Bullen used to ride a famous horse whose initials were O.N. Who was he?
10 Has Frank Weldon ever won the Badminton Horse Trials?

Eventing 4

1 At what time of the year do the Burghley Horse Trials take place?
2 Can you name the company which sponsors Burghley?
3 Who organizes Burghley?

4 Who won the Burghley Horse Trials on Priceless in 1983 and Night Cap in 1984?

5 On which horse did Captain Mark Phillips win the Burghley Horse Trials in 1973? The animal's initials were M.M.

6 Has Burghley ever staged a World Championship or a European Championship?

7 Who was the Marquess associated with Burghley?

8 Where are the Burghley Horse Trials held?

9 In which county is that?

10 Anneli Drummond-Hay won Burghley in 1961 on a famous horse with a hint of royalty about it. What was it called?

Eventing 5

1 Who is the only event rider to have won the World Championship twice?

2 What nationality is he?

3 Name the Briton who has won three Olympic gold medals – two team and one individual.

4 Has Captain Mark Phillips ever won an Olympic gold medal?

5 Who rode Cornishman V to win the 1970 World Championship in Punchestown?

6 Lester Piggott has a daughter who rides eventing. What is her name?

7 Who won the individual gold medal at the Los Angeles Olympics in 1984?

8 Where does he come from?

9 What are the horse trials called which are organized by Captain Mark Phillips?

10 Former event rider Chris Collins used to be a jockey. Under which rules did he ride?

Eventing 6

1 Under what governing body in this country do horse trials come?
2 Where is its base?
3 Mike Tucker is a rider and show organizer. Does he also commentate?
4 When did Princess Anne win the European Championship?
5 Where did she win the title?
6 Which horse did she ride?
7 Four years later she won a silver medal in the European Championships on another horse. What was it called?
8 In which country are the 1986 World Horse Trials Championships to be held?
9 Complete this rider's name: Diana C_____.
10 Which horse did she ride in the 1984 Los Angeles Olympics?

Eventing 7

1 Where were the 1973 European Championships held, in which Princess Anne rode and fell?
2 Princess Anne is president of which horse trials?
3 Who is the young lady who rides Running Bear and whose initials are K.S.?
4 Lord and Lady Hugh Russell used to run which horse trials?
5 In the past this man was chef d'équipe of British teams – Malcolm _____.
6 He was also a soldier in a famous horse regiment. Which one?
7 The first year Gatcombe Park Horse Trials were staged a husband and wife dead-heated for first place and had to be divided by a dressage mark. Who are they?
8 Regal Realm started life in which country?
9 Complete this rider's name: Rachel B_____?
10 Who is the rider associated with Gurgle The Greek?

Eventing 8

1 What nationality is Bill Roycroft?
2 Who rides Classic Lines?
3 In what Olympic Games did Princess Anne ride?
4 Did she win a medal?
5 Who won the team gold medal in the 1984 Los Angeles Olympics?
6 What medal did the British team win in those Games?
7 Who won the individual bronze for Britain?
8 What horse did she ride?
9 There was one man on the British team in Los Angeles. What was his name?
10 Why will Rachel Bayliss always remember Frauenfeld in 1983?

Eventing 9

1 What is the name of the end-of-season three-day event in Holland which begins with B?
2 What nationality is Mike Plumb?
3 What comes after the dressage and before the cross-country phase, which riders and their mounts have to jump?
4 Is time important in this particular section?
5 In which country are the Luhmühlen horse trials held?
6 Where is Locko Park?
7 What major event is staged there?
8 Which country has the most lady competitors?
9 Lady Victoria Leatham is president of which horse trials?
10 What are these horse trials called: Os_____?

Eventing 10

1 Can a horse take part in a three-day event if he is four years old?
2 At what age can a horse take part in horse trials?
3 At what age do riders become eligible to take part in the Junior European Horse Trials Championships?
4 When are they too old to ride in the Junior European Championships?
5 How old must a rider be to ride in the Young Riders' European Championships?
6 When is a rider too old to compete in young riders' events?
7 What phases make up a one-day event?
8 What phases make up the speed and endurance test in a three-day event?
9 By what nickname is Diana Clapham usually known?
10 Who sponsors the major championships at Locko Park in Derbyshire?

Dressage 1

1 Where are the dressage championships held in Sussex?
2 Which English lady rider has won more British Championships than any other?
3 What is the name of her most successful horse?
4 Where did they finish in the 1978 World Championship?
5 What relation is Jane Wilson to Christopher Bartle?
6 Which horse did Christopher Bartle ride in the 1984 Los Angeles Olympics?
7 Was his the best British Olympic placing ever?
8 Which horse did Jennie Loriston-Clark ride in the Los Angeles Games?
9 Who was the reserve rider for the British team at those Games?
10 What is her mount called with the initial S_____?

Dressage 2

1 Which Swiss lady rider was formerly Olympic, World and European Champion?
2 What is the name of her great horse which begins with G_____?
3 Who won the individual gold medal in the Los Angeles Olympics?
4 In 1984 he gave a superb display of dressage at which British show?
5 Complete this German rider's name: Harry B_____.
6 Where is Germany's annual dressage show held? It begins with an A and showjumping competitions are also held there.
7 Who is the Austrian lady rider with the initials E.T.?
8 Where was the Alternative Olympic Dressage held in 1980?
9 What do the initials CDIO mean?
10 Complete this rider's name: Gabriela Gr_____.

Dressage 3

1 Which nation is considered to be the strongest at dressage?
2 What is the highest level competition dressage called?
3 Complete this movement: half p_____.
4 Can a pirouette be performed at a walk and a canter?
5 What does a rider do after entering the ring, before starting his test?
6 What does a rider do before leaving the ring?
7 Complete this movement: flying c_____.
8 When a horse goes from one pace to another it is called what?
9 Will a lack of rhythm cause a loss of marks?
10 There are five levels of British Horse Society dressage test. The first is preliminary. What are the others?

Horse racing 1

1 Where is the Derby run?
2 The Oaks is a race restricted to what?
3 What are the two classics held in the early part of the season at Newmarket?
4 What is the last classic race of the season which is run at Doncaster and sounds like a book?
5 Name the Derby winner who was kidnapped in 1983 and has never been found.
6 Who rode him to win the Derby?
7 Who has won the Epsom Derby more times than any other rider?
8 Who was Champion Flat jockey in 1984?
9 What nationality is he?
10 Complete this rider's name: Willie _____?

Horse racing 2

1 Where is the Grand National run?
2 Who was the famous steeplechaser who won the Grand National three times and whose initials are R. R.?
3 What is the biggest fence on the Grand National course?
4 How long is the Grand National?
5 Where are the Champion Hurdle and the Gold Cup staged?
6 In racing terms what is another name for grass?
7 What are the shirts which jockeys wear called?
8 Who is the member of the Royal family closely associated with Flat racing and who owns many horses?
9 Where is the headquarters of British racing?
10 At which racecourse in Berkshire do the men wear toppers and tails and some of the ladies outrageous hats?

Pony Club 1

1   Which Scottish branch of the Pony Club, whose name begins with E, won the Prince Philip Cup for the Pony Club Mounted Games Championship three times in succession from 1982 to 1984?

2   Where is the final of this Championship held?

3   Where is the headquarters of the Pony Club?

4   Name one of the games which has the initials S.S.D.?

5   Who is the well-known man who does the commentating for the Mounted Games?

6   How many teams actually take part in the competition on the final evening?

7   What, apart from colours and jodphurs, must all competitors wear?

8   Is the scoring done with faults or points?

9   What does it mean to compete *hors concours*?

10   One famous Pony Club team had to compete *hors concours* in the Championship in 1984. What was that team's name?

Other equestrian sport 1

1 Which member of the Royal family regularly plays polo?
2 Where is Cowdray Park?
3 Did Prince Philip ever play polo?
4 What sport does Prince Philip regularly take part in now?
5 Who owns the horses he uses?
6 Name the man, whose initials are J.P., who drives the Norwich Union coach.
7 In 1984 he broke the record for driving a coach non-stop – from where to London?
8 Which famous British coach driver has the initials G.B.?
9 What are the obstacles placed in the main arena during the coach and carriage driving competitions?
10 What country beginning with Hu_____ has produced a World Driving Champion?

Other equestrian sport 2

1 Are point-to-point meetings held in England on a Sunday?
2 What is the type of point-to-point race beginning with O?
3 Complete this point-to-point rider's name: David T_____.
4 When does the point-to-point season start?
5 What is the well-known point-to-point course in Kent which carries the first name of a railway station?
6 Do professional riders or amateurs compete in point-to-point races?
7 Do point-to-point horses start from stalls?
8 Complete this point-to-point course's name: Twes_____.
9 Where is the Ashford Valley point-to-point held?
10 Is there a hunter championship race held at Chepstow?

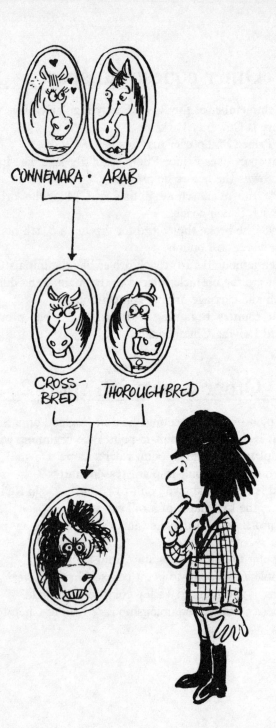

CONNEMARA · ARAB

CROSS-BRED   THOROUGHBRED

Breeds 1

1 What breed of pony comes from the Hampshire area?
2 What is the smallest breed of horse in the world?
3 What famous breed of pony comes from Scotland?
4 Name the two breeds of ponies who come from the West Country.
5 What breed of pony was used at the 1984 Olympic Christmas show over a mini Grand National course?
6 Complete this American breed of horse: T_____ W_____ Horse.
7 What is the term commonly used for breeds such as the Shire and Clydesdale?
8 Name the breed of horse which is noted for its good looks and stamina, and which originates from the East.
9 What breed of horse was English racing originally based on?
10 What is the place called where horses are bred?

Breeds 2

1 From which country does the Andalusian come?
2 What is the name of the famous heavy-horse breed which comes from France and begins with P?
3 A Trakehner comes from where?
4 Which British breed is noted for its high-stepping action?
5 Where does the Pindos come from?
6 Name the German-bred horse whose name begins with Ha which many showjumpers ride?
7 Does the Oldenburg come from the same country?
8 What is the distinctive marking of the Appaloosa?
9 Does the Haflinger come from Iceland or Austria?
10 Where does the Connemara pony come from?

Organizations 1

1 Complete this name: the A_____ H_____ Society.
2 The Association of British R_____ S_____.
3 British Ap_____ S_____.
4 British Show P_____ S_____.
5 Shire H_____ S_____.
6 Worshipful Company of S_____.
7 Dales P_____ S_____.
8 Exmoor P_____ S_____.
9 Fell P_____ S_____.
10 What do these initials stand for: HHS?

Organizations 2

1 British V_____ A_____.
2 Master of F_____ A_____.
3 Racehorse O_____ A_____.
4 Royal Ag_____ S_____ of E_____.
5 Society of M_____ S_____.
6 Shetland P_____ S_____ S_____.
7 Western H_____ A_____ of G_____ B_____.
8 Suf_____ H_____ S_____.
9 Pon_____ of B_____.
10 Hurlingham P_____ A_____.

Organizations 3

1 British S_____ P_____ Society.
2 C_____ Pony Breeders Society.
3 Do_____ Breed Society.
4 High_____ Pony Society.
5 Home of _____ _____ _____.
6 S_____ S_____ Association.
7 London Harn_____ Horse P_____ Society.
8 Royal C_____ of V_____ S_____.
9 British Tr_____ Association.
10 British Pal_____ Society.

Miscellaneous 1

1 Name the horse who was ridden by Alexander the Great.
2 Who was the horse Napoleon rode at the battle of Waterloo?
3 Name the famous eighteenth-century artist renowned for his paintings of horses, whose surname begins with S?
4 If a piece of red ribbon is tied to a hunter's tail, what does that denote?
5 If a horse wears a white ribbon on its tail, what does that denote?
6 Should a horse who wears a red ribbon on its tail be at the front, middle or back of the hunt?
7 What is the title given to the person who controls the hounds?
8 A British high-jump record of 7 feet $7^5/_{16}$ inches was set in 1978. Who by (horse and rider)?
9 What is the world high-jump record and when was it set?
10 Name one of the oldest known games, a form of which was played in 525 BC.

Miscellaneous 2

1 What is considered to be the fastest horse in the world over short distances?
2 Kentucky is sometimes known as the _____ country.
3 What American racehorse has won more prize money than any other? He is a gelding and has the initials J. H.
4 What was the name of the horse that cowboy Roy Rogers used to ride?
5 What is a show called, particularly in America, where the riders partner bucking broncos and bulls?

6   Complete the name of this place in Canada where many horse activities take place: Cal_____.
7   What is the horse sport called, where the runners must not break into a canter or a gallop?
8   Do the jockeys ride the horses in that sport?
9   What is the name of the famous race run in Czechoslovakia which begins with the letter P_____?
10 Is it a flat race?

Miscellaneous 3

1   From what country do the Carmargue horses come?
2   What was the name given to the equines who worked down mines?
3   What do you call it when you are going fast on a horse or pony?
4   Name the famous novel by Anna Sewell.
5   Napoleon fought Wellington at the battle of Waterloo. What was the name of Wellington's horse?
6   When a person is learning to ride he or she is known as a nov_____.
7   What is the name for officers of the law who ride horses?
8   When you ride a horse without a saddle what do you call it?
9   What is the name for a place where you ride under cover?
10 Where is the Spanish Riding School?

Miscellaneous 4

1 What are the men called who ride horses and carry a lance in the bullring?
2 What is the term for a male horse who stands at stud?
3 What is the name of the military horse who was badly injured in a London bomb attack in 1982?
4 What is the name given to the person who does the selling of horses and ponies at sales?
5 When several people want to buy the same horse at the sales what do they do against each other?
6 Who puts up the jumps at a show?
7 What are people who look after horses and ponies called?
8 What is an AI?
9 What operation makes a male horse into a gelding?
10 If your mare cannot produce foals, it means she is what?

Miscellaneous 5

1 General Custer used to chase the Indians with his mounted troops called?
2 The Indians used to call them Horse S_____.
3 Complete this phrase: The Charge of the _____.
4 Complete this quotation: 'A horse! A horse! My _____.'
5 What was the famous wooden horse in history beginning with T?
6 Throughout the ages children have ridden horses made of wood. What are those horses called?
7 Name the minuscule sea creature with an equine name.
8 What do children traditionally ride on the beach at the seaside?
9 What is the emblem of Lloyds Bank?
10 Is the horse a herd animal?

Miscellaneous 6

1 What is the name for a horse doctor?
2 What was the first known horse called?
3 It progressed and became what it is today because of ev_____.
4 The wild horses of the prairies in America are known as M_____.
5 Who is the man who used to be a National Hunt jockey and now writes best-selling novels? His initials are D.F.
6 What is the rope called which cowboys use to catch horses and cattle?
7 Cowboys do not wear jodphurs, but many do cover their legs with leather c_____?
8 What is the name given to the wild horses in rodeos: b_____
9 Complete this saying: Horses for _____.
10 When the knights of old used to ride against each other for the hand of a fair maiden, what was it called?

Miscellaneous 7

1 What is a hunter called who is up to carrying a lot of weight?
2 What is the French for horse?
3 What is the German for horse?
4 What were the robbers on horseback called who held up stagecoaches in the old days?
5 Name the infamous one whose first name was Dick.
6 What was the name of his horse?
7 If you pay for your horse to be looked after by someone else, it is known as being at l_____.

8 Who is the well-known retailer of horse clothes and equipment with the initials H.H.?
9 When a horse has never had a saddle or bridle on him before and he is intended for riding, what must happen to him before he will ever be ridden properly?
10 We call them stables, but the Americans call them b_____.

Miscellaneous 8

1 Is a polo pony allowed to wear blinkers?
2 What do polo players hit the ball with?
3 What does a polo player have to wear on his head?
4 Which of our kings started the wearing of the velvet hunting cap?
5 What was the name of the horse who was supposed to have wings?
6 At which state occasion does the Queen ride side-saddle down the Mall?
7 Name the authors of *The Irish R.M.*
8 A jockey rides a racehorse, but what is the person called who teaches the animal its job?
9 With what game would you associate the word chukka?
10 With what sport would you associate the words roads and tracks?

Miscellaneous 9

1 Where does the annual Golden Horseshoe Ride final take place?

2 In the sport of carriage driving, into what are the scores converted?

3 There are three phases in top level carriage driving. What are they?

4 Prince Philip, George Bowman and Peter M_____ won a bronze medal in the 1981 World Driving Championships. What is Peter's surname?

5 Should you water a horse before or after feeding?

6 Complete this title: 'Approved R_____ S_____.

7 Would you now connect Miss Diana Mason with showjumping, dressage or eventing?

8 This man was Chairman of the British Horse Society's Pony Club for years. Complete his name: Major W. J. P_____.

9 When does membership of the Pony Club end for each member?

10 Complete this former eventing gold-medal winner's name: Major Derek Al_____.

Answers

Stable management 1

1 Manger or haynet.
2 Bedding.
3 Slight slope.
4 Mucking out.
5 Grooming.

6 Dandy brush.
7 No.
8 Hoof pick.
9 A rug and perhaps blankets.
10 Rectum.

Stable management 2

1 Rasping.
2 Farrier/blacksmith.
3 Hoof pick (the other two are grooming brushes).
4 Foot.
5 Four.
6 Weaving.

7 Near-fore.
8 Disease of the frog.
9 To develop and harden muscle and to promote circulation.
10 Pastern.

Stable management 3

1 Teeth.
2 Yearling.
3 Stallion.
4 Mane.
5 Hands.

6 Soft.
7 By the teeth.
8 'No foot – no horse'.
9 Super-chilled marker.
10 Colt.

Stable management 4

1 Yes, because he could panic, break it and possibly hurt himself.
2 On the fetlocks.
3 Gelding.
4 14.2hh.
5 'Good doer'.
6 Hot and cold.

7 Farrier/blacksmith.
8 No. It should be secured by a string loop which is attached to the stable ring, so that he can pull away without injuring himself.
9 Salt-lick.
10 100.5°F.

Stable management 5

1 Outside, for safety.
2 No, the seeds and dust could drop into his eyes.
3 Drainage.
4 Safety knot.
5 To help keep them in good condition, for appearance, and to promote growth.
6 Wheat, oat, barley.
7 Wheat straw – the horse is less likely to eat it.
8 Skep.
9 Muck hill (or heap).
10 Roller.

Stable management 6

1 No, it could affect the horse's blood circulation.
2 To protect the hairs at the top of the tail.
3 Clean it and store it carefully.
4 Curry comb.
5 Drying ears and polishing coat.
6 Pick out feet.
7 Straw or hay.
8 No, it could split the hairs or pull them out.
9 To one side, so he cannot kick you.
10 Sponge them.

Stable management 7

1 4 feet.
2 So that the pony can look out, and for ventilation.
3 Outside.
4 Setting fair.
5 Clipping.
6 Pulling.
7 Hogged.
8 Bran mash.
9 Lengthways.
10 To prevent choking.

Stable management 8

1 Tin, otherwise food could get wet or damp. Tin also protects it from rats and mice.
2 Farrier/blacksmith.
3 Cast.
4 Studs.
5 Nails and their clenches.
6 Forging.
7 Yes.
8 Fork, barrow (or sack), hard broom.
9 To air and dry.
10 Every day.

Stable management 9

1 Top of the withers.
2 Full clip.
3 Usually between four and six weeks.
4 In case the horse gets cast.
5 Stall.
6 Yes.
7 Stallion.
8 Chopped hay.
9 Yes.
10 Yes.

Stable management 10

1 To relax them.
2 Type of bedding (where droppings are removed, fresh bedding put on top of existing bedding to save labour).
3 On the flat of the hand.
4 Shape and appearance.
5 Right.
6 Teeth.
7 Windsucker.
8 South.
9 40 or 42.
10 Strapping.

Grass-kept horses and ponies 1

1 Ragwort.
2 Four, one for each horse.
3 Dry him off.
4 New Zealand.
5 Remove the mud.
6 So that he retains his body oils for protection against the weather.
7 Headcollar or halter.
8 Tit-bit.
9 Shelter.
10 Before removing headcollar, shut the gate for safety.

Grass-kept horses and ponies 2

1 Yes, because the feet still grow.
2 Break the ice regularly.
3 One who lives out to give him extra protection against the elements.
4 Laminitis.
5 Rotational grazing.
6 Removing droppings from the field regularly.
7 Yes.
8 To examine him and also to get him used to being caught.
9 No.
10 Lice and deterioration in condition.

Grass-kept horses and ponies 3

1 Barbed wire.
2 Yes.
3 They reduce the worm parasites.
4 To see if the rug has slipped and to check his general condition.
5 Re-proof it.
6 No, he might get it caught up in something.
7 Rustlers.
8 At least one acre.
9 Put it in piles, more piles than there are horses.
10 To save arguments and to make sure each gets some.

Grass-kept horses and ponies 4

1 Yes.
2 Pull it up by the roots and then burn it.
3 Ears and loins.
4 That the entrance is wide enough for at least two horses to pass each other; and it should face away from the prevailing wind.
5 By putting down straw on the floor and hanging a haynet.
6 Pick them up and remove them – they are poisonous to horses.
7 Keep the flies at bay.
8 Electric fencing.
9 The rug slipping sideways and the back of it rucking up.
10 Usually canvas.

Grass-kept horses and ponies 5

1 To pick up any dangerous objects such as bottles or bricks.
2 Yes, provided it's clean but you must also have a water tank in the field for him to drink from.
3 Slip the headcollar off gently and do not encourage him to gallop off, because he might stumble and hurt himself. He might also get excited, kick and injure his handler.
4 Because he might not like his new home at first and might break out and return to his old home.
5 To make sure he is alright, has all he needs and that nobody is trying to steal him.
6 Separate him from the one who is causing the trouble and, if possible, put him with a horse who does not mind his company.
7 In case he has been bitten

or has knocked or cut himself.

8 Hay.
9 No, dry him off and then turn him out, otherwise he might catch a cold.
10 Because your horse or pony might hurt himself and need veterinary attention as quickly as possible. If you did not have it with you, you could waste valuable time.

Saddlery 1

1 Tack.
2 Saddle soap or occasionally neatsfoot oil.
3 Two.
4 Stuben.
5 A crop.
6 Whip (crop).
7 Pommel.
8 Stirrup leathers.
9 Cantle.
10 Stirrup bars.

Saddlery 2

1 Stirrup irons.
2 Thick rubber band.
3 Have it restuffed.
4 Gullet.
5 Broken tree.
6 Spring tree saddle.
7 Safety catches.
8 Numnah.
9 Girth.
10 Well fitting.

Saddlery 3

1 Tepid.
2 No, the leather would crack.
3 For wear and tear.
4 Tack room.
5 Saddle horse.
6 Snaffle, curb and Pelham.
7 Headband (or headpiece).
8 A bit.
9 Small piece of leather, with rings on either side, attached to the bridle.
10 Throatlash (or throatlatch).

Saddlery 4

1 Standing, running, Irish.
2 A girth.
3 A bit.
4 A bitless bridle.
5 To prevent the horse opening his mouth.
6 Girth.
7 To stop the saddle slipping back.
8 To stop the saddle slipping forward.
9 Noseband.
10 Crossed noseband.

Riding technique 1

1 Three.
2 Near-fore.
3 Extended trot.
4 Four.
5 Sideways.
6 Aids.
7 Collected walk.
8 Working, medium, collected, extended.
9 Two.
10 Changing legs; possibly a flying change.

Riding technique 2

1 To make the horse supple and obedient.
2 Reining back.
3 Refusal.
4 Cavalletti.
5 Tracking up.
6 Calling a cab.
7 Collected and balanced.
8 Transition.
9 Resistance.
10 Walk.

Riding technique 3

1 In.
2 Pecking.
3 Cat-jumping.
4 Running out.
5 No – it should bend.
6 Over-jumping.
7 He gets close to a fence by putting in an extra stride, not required by the rider, before taking off.
8 Down.
9 No.
10 Neck strap.

Before and after a ride 1

1 Yes.
2 His feet and shoes.
3 Run them up or cross them over the saddle.
4 Girths.
5 Hard hat.
6 Safety harness.
7 Protect your head.
8 No.
9 So he does not slip.
10 No – it's unorthodox and the horse may run off with you.

Before and after a ride 2

1 Place your fingertips on the buckle and the iron under your armpit.
2 Level and not twisted.
3 Left (when facing the same direction as the horse).
4 Leg-up.
5 Twisted or slack.
6 Mounting block.
7 Level, and neither too high nor too low.
8 Tight (or too loose).
9 Towards the tail.
10 Three: foot in stirrup iron, impulsion up to saddle, sit in saddle.

Before and after a ride 3

1 Dry him off.
2 No.
3 Yes.
4 Thatching.
5 Bit.
6 To look for cuts.
7 Bucket of fresh water.
8 No – he might catch cold: dry him.
9 Headcollar or halter.
10 New Zealand rug. (Some native ponies, however, can withstand the elements without this rug.)

Safety 1

1 Left.
2 Young horse.
3 Fluorescent, reflective tabards.
4 Correct lights – white facing to the front, red to the rear.
5 Shoulder height.
6 Right hand up, palm of hand facing forward.
7 One horse's length.
8 Bridle.
9 Get off and lead the horse.
10 In single file.

Safety 2

1 No, it breaks concentration.
2 Continually lower right arm from waist high to side.
3 Halt and look both ways.
4 No, it is sloppy and dangerous. Your horse must be under full control at all times.
5 Put your left arm out at shoulder height.
6 Nod your head and thank them.
7 No, your horse might slip.
8 Dismount and lead.
9 Dismount and lead.
10 It is dangerous: your horse might run out into the traffic.

Safety 3

1 The Highway Code.
2 Yes.
3 Shut it.
4 Shy away from it.
5 Keep to the edges, or 'headlands'.
6 Keep to bridlepaths.
7 People and dogs.
8 To avoid being kicked.
9 Courteously and considerately.
10 Clear signals.

Safety 4

1 On the left, with yourself between the horse and the traffic.
2 A bridle: it is dangerous (and against the law) to do otherwise.
3 Wrap them around your hands – if your horse ran off he might drag you.
4 No; he should be schooled with an experienced horse on minor roads, where there is very little traffic, so that he can get used to it.
5 Say you cannot stop unless it is vital, because your horse might become restless and either step into the traffic or back into it. Keep moving.
6 No: the pavement is for pedestrians, not horses; only ride on the pavement in an emergency.
7 No, the rider signals his intentions to turn right, but keeps to the nearside until he reaches the centre of the junction and then, when all is clear, he makes for the nearside of the road he is turning into.
8 Always keep to the outside of a roundabout because it is safer.
9 Always walk, otherwise the horse you are passing might be startled.
10 Absolutely not: it is highly dangerous not to give your full attention to what you are doing.

Ailments 1

1 Thrush.
2 Neglect, for instance, to allow the horse to stand continuously in an improperly mucked-out stable.
3 Corns.
4 Colic.
5 Abscess on the poll caused by pressure or a blow.
6 Mud fever.
7 Laminitis.
8 In the feet.
9 The wall of the feet.
10 Worms.

Ailments 2

1 Red worm.
2 Isolate him.
3 First-aid kit.
4 A skin condition, particularly affecting the mane and tail areas.
5 A soft swelling on the inside, and to the front of, the hock.
6 Over-reach.
7 Stringhalt.
8 Tubing.
9 A whistler or a roarer.
10 A gelding.

Ailments 3

1 Pedalostitis.
2 Galloping on hard ground.
3 Swellings just above and on either side of the fetlock.
4 Anti-tetanus.
5 Yes, they can, several types.
6 Ringworm.
7 In the mouth.
8 A fly; a small lump on a horse's back, caused by the larva of the warble fly.
9 The nose and throat.
10 Gadfly larvae.

Ailments 4

1 A bony enlargement on the leg.
2 In the foot.
3 Because the feet grow continually and need regular trimming, and the shoes wear out and if not changed will cause lameness.
4 In the foot.
5 Complete rest.
6 Deep ridges appear around it.
7 Yes, and if the foot is tapped it is very painful for him.
8 Isolate him.
9 The muscles of the loins.
10 Bread or bran soaked in water.

Travelling 1

1 Travelling boots or bandages.

2 A poll guard to protect the top of his head.

3 Make arrangements to give him food and water and a chance to get out and stretch his legs.

4 Yes, in case water is not available there.

5 Because it takes only a fraction of the time and he will not suffer any loss of condition.

6 A tranquillizer.

7 Plenty of room and light, padded partitions and anti-slip floors.

8 Tail guard or bandage.

9 You must not tie it on too tight, nor leave it on for long periods.

10 No – he will almost certainly catch a chill.

Travelling 2

1 The ramp.

2 Make sure it is level on the ground.

3 Facing the car that is pulling it.

4 Try him with a bucket of food, or put straw down on the ramp, in case it is frightening him, and make sure there is a light inside.

5 A lunge line – gradually increasing the pressure with it as he walks forward.

6 Park the box or trailer so that the ramp has a wall one side and get your helpers to stand on the other side.

7 With care – the driver must not put himself in a position where he has to brake quickly because the horse might hurt itself.

8 No, it is highly dangerous and illegal.

9 Anti-sweat rug.

10 A haynet.

Vices 1

1 Bolting.

2 Rearing.

3 A rack chain; or use two ropes, each tied to a different tie ring in the wall, so that he cannot reach the knot of either rope.

4 Douse the bedding with a weak solution of disinfectant.

5 Give him a light tap on the nose and say 'No' sharply.

6 Boredom.

7 Because they are a herd animal and like being with other horses or animals.

8 Roll.

9 Your temper.

10 A muzzle.

Food 1

1 Boil it well, otherwise it can be poisonous.
2 Often.
3 It adds bulk to the feed and ensures the horse chews properly.
4 After hard exercise, or if your horse is unwell (it is easily digested and acts as a laxative).
5 They make them 'hot' (excited).
6 Remove it – never leave stale food in a manger.
7 All 'hard' feed.
8 Hay.
9 Sweet – then you know it is good.
10 Very small in comparison with his body size.

Food 2

1 Soak it in water overnight – fed dry it could swell in the horse's stomach and give him colic.
2 Yes, and also heating (to the blood).
3 Split or crush them.
4 Grasses.
5 Grass.
6 Hay.
7 Gradually, so as not to upset his system.
8 Clean it out for hygiene reasons.
9 Proteins and vitamins.
10 No, he must be given time to digest his food.

Showjumping 1

1 1970.
2 No.
3 Robert and Steven.
4 Steven.
5 Team silver.
6 Ronnie Massarella.
7 Peter Robeson.
8 Ryan's Son.
9 Lieutenant John Ledingham.
10 Boomerang.

Showjumping 2

1 1984.
2 Raymond Brooks-Ward.
3 Indoor.
4 Douglas Bunn.
5 Three.
6 Derby Bank.
7 Ted Edgar.
8 Nick Skelton.
9 Marion Mould (née Coakes).
10 Wembley.

Showjumping 3

1 Malcolm Pyrah.
2 Yes.
3 Gatcombe Park.
4 Irish.
5 Liz Edgar.
6 Ted Edgar.
7 Park Farm Arena, Northwood, Middlesex.
8 Four.
9 Hickstead.
10 Pat Koechlin-Smythe.

Showjumping 4

1 West German.
2 Roman.
3 Aachen.
4 Ann Moore.
5 Munich.
6 Harvey Smith.
7 Yorkshire.
8 Australian (Jeff McVean).
9 David Broome.
10 Sanyo.

Showjumping 5

1 Marius.
2 Nick Skelton.
3 7 feet 7⁵/₁₆ inches.
4 Lastic.
5 Dorian Williams.
6 Canada.
7 United States of America.
8 Hans Winkler.
9 Yorkshire.
10 Showjumping fence.

Showjumping 6

1 Eight faults.
2 Scotland.
3 Fédération Equestre Internationale.
4 The Royal International Horse Show.
5 Michael Mac.
6 Kelly and Emma Brown.
7 Stephen Hadley.
8 Collecting ring.
9 Julia Longland.
10 Bath and West.

Showjumping 7

1 Pavarotti.
2 The Edgars' Everest Stud.
3 Austrian.
4 Australia.
5 Lieutenant-Commander Bill Jefferies.
6 Maureen Holden.
7 Seoul, South Korea.
8 Bronze.
9 Abdullah.
10 Hendrik Snoek.

Showjumping 8

1 Ireland.
2 Donaueschingen.
3 Detling.
4 Dorian Williams.
5 1900.
6 Jean Germany.
7 Philco.
8 Boysie and Brindle Boy.
9 Lancashire.
10 Stoneleigh, Warwickshire.

Showjumping 9

1 Heidi Robbiani.
2 American.
3 Five.
4 West Germany.
5 Alwin and Paul Schockemöhle.
6 Next.
7 Belgian.
8 Beethoven.
9 Three.
10 Edgar.

Showjumping 10

1 The Horse of the Year show is staged indoors, while Hickstead is an outdoor arena.
2 Hugo Simon.
3 West Germany.
4 Italy.
5 Nations Cup.
6 Four.
7 The Prince Philip Cup (formerly the President's Cup).
8 The Maverick.
9 Alison Dawes (after her marriage, Westwood before).
10 Take Your Own Line.

Showjumping 11

1 Colonel Sir Michael Ansell.
2 Yes – there is a time allowed, a time limit (twice the time allowed), timed jumps-off and speed classes.
3 Italy.
4 Ted Williams.
5 United States of America.
6 Puissance.
7 No, but they used to.
8 Mark and Philip Heffer.
9 Fire.
10 Norwich Union.

Showjumping 12

1 Dinard, France.
2 Foxhunter.
3 Nick Skelton.
4 No, it was Malcolm Pyrah.
5 Olympia.
6 Moët et Chandon.
7 Everest.
8 Ann Moore.
9 Three.
10 Berlin.

Showjumping 13

1 Alan Smith.
2 BBC.
3 Three Counties.
4 Essex.
5 Michael Whitaker.
6 Yes (in 1984).
7 Yes.
8 General Sir Cecil Blacker.
9 Peter Luther.
10 French.

Eventing 1

1 Penalty points.
2 Dressage.
3 Showjumping.
4 Veterinary inspection.
5 Spun.
6 Twenty penalties.
7 Three.
8 0.25 penalty for each second over.
9 Reverse.
10 Avon.

Eventing 2

1 1949.
2 Frank Weldon.
3 Lucinda Green.
4 Six.
5 Prior-Palmer.
6 Be Fair.
7 David Green.
8 Regal Realm.
9 SR Direct Mail.
10 Her Majesty The Queen.

Eventing 3

1 Mrs Waddington.
2 Columbus.
3 Four.
4 Speculator III.
5 Richard Walker.

6 Beaufort.
7 Whitbread.
8 Mark Todd.
9 Our Nobby.
10 Yes, in 1956 on Kilbarry.

Eventing 4

1 September.
2 Remy Martin.
3 Charles Stratton.
4 Virginia Holgate.
5 Maid Marion.

6 Yes, both.
7 Exeter.
8 Stamford.
9 Lincolnshire.
10 Merely-a-Monarch.

Eventing 5

1 Bruce Davidson.
2 American.
3 Richard Meade.
4 Yes, he won a team gold medal in the Munich Olympics in 1972.

5 Mary Gordon Watson.
6 Maureen.
7 Mark Todd.
8 New Zealand.
9 Gatcombe Park.
10 National Hunt rules.

Eventing 6

1 British Horse Society.
2 British Equestrian Centre, Stoneleigh, Warwickshire.
3 Yes.
4 1971.
5 Burghley.

6 Doublet.
7 Goodwill.
8 Australia.
9 Diana Clapham.
10 Windjammer.

Eventing 7

1 Kiev.
2 Windsor.
3 Karen Straker.
4 Wylye.
5 Malcolm Wallace.

6 The King's Troop.
7 Lucinda and David Green.
8 Australia.
9 Rachel Bayliss.
10 Rachel Bayliss.

Eventing 8

1 Australian.
2 Mark Phillips.
3 Montreal.
4 No: she finished 24th on Goodwill.
5 The Americans.
6 A silver medal.
7 Virginia Holgate.
8 Priceless.
9 Ian Stark.
10 She won the European Championship.

Eventing 9

1 Boekelo.
2 American.
3 Steeplechase course.
4 Yes.
5 West Germany.
6 Derbyshire.
7 The Midland Bank Championships (National Championships).
8 Britain.
9 Burghley.
10 Osberton.

Eventing 10

1 No – he must be six or over.
2 Five or over.
3 Riders are eligible from the beginning of the year of their fourteenth birthday.
4 After the end of the year of their eighteenth birthday.
5 Nineteen.
6 After the end of their twenty-first year.
7 Dressage, showjumping, cross-country.
8 Phases (a) roads and tracks, (b) steeplechase, (c) roads and tracks, (d) cross-country.
9 Tiny.
10 Midland Bank.

Dressage 1

1 Goodwood.
2 Jennie Loriston-Clark.
3 Dutch Courage.
4 Third.
5 Sister.
6 Wily Trout.
7 Yes.
8 Prince Consort.
9 Tanya Larrigan.
10 Salute.

Dressage 2

1 Christine Stückelberger.
2 Granat.
3 Reiner Klimke.
4 Horse of the Year Show, Wembley.
5 Harry Boldt.
6 Aachen.
7 Elisabeth Theurer.
8 Goodwood.
9 Concours de Dressage International Officiel.
10 Gabriela Grillo.

Dressage 3

1 West Germany.
2 Grand Prix.
3 Half pass.
4 Yes.
5 Salute the judges.
6 Salute the judges.
7 Flying change.
8 A transition.
9 Yes.
10 Novice, Elementary, Medium and Advanced.

Horse racing 1

1 Epsom.
2 Fillies.
3 1000 and 2000 Guineas.
4 St Leger.
5 Shergar.
6 Walter Swinburn.
7 Lester Piggott.
8 Steve Cauthen.
9 American.
10 Carson.

Horse racing 2

1 Aintree, Liverpool.
2 Red Rum.
3 The Chair.
4 Four-and-a-half miles.
5 Cheltenham.
6 Turf.
7 Colours or silks.
8 The Queen.
9 Newmarket.
10 Royal Ascot.

Pony Club 1

1 Eglinton.
2 The Horse of the Year Show, Wembley.
3 Stoneleigh, Warwickshire.
4 Stepping Stone Dash.
5 Raymond Brooks-Ward.
6 Four.
7 A hard hat.
8 Points.
9 To compete without score counting.
10 Atherstone.

Other equestrian sport 1

1 Prince Charles.
2 Sussex.
3 Yes.
4 Carriage driving.
5 Her Majesty The Queen.
6 John Parker.
7 Bristol.
8 George Bowman.
9 Cones.
10 Hungary.

Other equestrian sport 2

1 No.
2 Open.
3 David Turner.
4 February.
5 Charing.
6 Amateurs.
7 No.
8 Tweseldown.
9 Charing.
10 Yes.

Breeds 1

1 New Forest.
2 Falabella.
3 Shetland.
4 Dartmoor and Exmoor.
5 Shetland.
6 Tennessee Walking Horse.
7 Heavy horses.
8 Arab horse.
9 Arab.
10 Stud.

Breeds 2

1 Spain.
2 Percheron.
3 Originally East Prussia.
4 Hackney.
5 Greece.
6 Hanoverian.
7 Yes.
8 Spots.
9 Austria.
10 Ireland.

Organizations 1

1 Arab Horse Society.
2 Association of British Riding Schools.
3 British Appaloosa Society.
4 British Show Pony Society.
5 Shire Horse Society.
6 Worshipful Company of Saddlers.
7 Dales Pony Society.
8 Exmoor Pony Society.
9 Fell Pony Society.
10 Hackney Horse Society.

Organizations 2

1 British Veterinary Association.
2 Master of Foxhounds Association.
3 Racehorse Owners Association.
4 Royal Agriculture Society of England.
5 Society of Master Saddlers.
6 Shetland Pony Studbook Society.
7 Western Horsemen's Association of Great Britain.
8 Suffolk Horse Society.
9 Ponies of Britain.
10 Hurlingham Polo Association.

Organizations 3

1 British Spotted Pony Society.
2 Connemara Pony Breeders Society.
3 Donkey Breed Society.
4 Highland Pony Society.
5 Home of Rest for Horses.
6 Side Saddle Association.
7 London Harness Horse Parade Society.
8 Royal College of Veterinary Surgeons.
9 British Trakehner Association.
10 British Palomino Society.

Miscellaneous 1

1 Bucephalus.
2 Marengo.
3 George Stubbs.
4 The horse kicks.
5 He is a novice.
6 Back.
7 Huntsman.
8 Nick Skelton riding Lastic.
9 8 feet 1½ inches set in 1949 (by Captain Alberto Larraguibel of Chile riding Huaso).
10 Polo.

Miscellaneous 2

1 American Quarter Horse.
2 Blue Grass Country.
3 John Henry.
4 Trigger.
5 Rodeo.
6 Calgary.
7 Trotting.
8 Generally no, but in France trotters and pacers are raced both in harness and under saddle.
9 Pardubice.
10 No, a steeplechase.

Miscellaneous 3

1 France.
2 Pit ponies.
3 A gallop.
4 *Black Beauty*.
5 Copenhagen.
6 Novice.
7 Mounted policemen and women.
8 Bareback riding.
9 Indoor school.
10 In Vienna, Austria.

Miscellaneous 4

1 Picadors.
2 A stallion.
3 Sefton.
4 Auctioneer.
5 Bid against each other.
6 The course builder.
7 Grooms, stablelads or stablegirls.
8 Assistant Instructor/Instructress (someone who has passed the British Horse Society's Assistant Instructor's examination).
9 Castration.
10 Barren.

Miscellaneous 5

1 Cavalry.
2 Horse Soldiers.
3 The Charge of The Light Brigade.
4 'A horse! A horse! My kingdom for a horse' (from *Richard III* by William Shakespeare).
5 The Trojan Horse.
6 Rocking horses.
7 Sea horse.
8 Donkeys.
9 A black horse.
10 Yes.

Miscellaneous 6

1 Vet (veterinary surgeon).
2 Eohippus.
3 Evolution.
4 Mustangs.
5 Dick Francis.
6 Lasso.
7 Chaps.
8 Bucking broncos.
9 Horses for courses.
10 Jousting.

Miscellaneous 7

1　Heavyweight hunter.
2　Cheval.
3　Pferd.
4　Highwaymen.
5　Dick Turpin.
6　Black Bess.

7　Livery.
8　Harry Hall.
9　He must be broken in, or backed.
10　Barns.

Miscellaneous 8

1　No.
2　Polo sticks or malets.
3　A helmet with a chin strap.
4　George III.
5　Pegasus.

6　Trooping the Colour.
7　Somerville and Ross.
8　The trainer.
9　Polo.
10　Eventing.

Miscellaneous 9

1　Exmoor.
2　Penalty points.
3　Presentation and dressage; marathon; obstacle driving.
4　Munt.
5　Before.
6　Approved Riding School.
7　Dressage.
8　Major W. J. Pinney.
9　When they reach twenty-one years of age.
10　Major Derek Allhusen, a member of the gold-medal winning team at the 1968 Mexico Olympics. He also won the individual silver medal at those Games and is now a top owner.